Happy Baking

Love Beccy x

Thank you for buying

*A Guide to Hosting Afternoon Tea
with Beccy's Favourite Recipes*

Please do support me and leave a review.

Beccy regularly hosts *Baking Demonstrations with Afternoon Tea* in her beautiful home. Scan the Qr below for more information.

(To scan the Qr code hold the camera on your smart phone over the Qr code and click then click the link that appears on your camera)

www.chezbeccy.com

A guide to hosting
AFTERNOON TEA
WITH BECCY'S FAVOURITE RECIPES

For Jim

www.chezbeccy.com

www.chezbeccy.com

A guide to hosting
AFTERNOON TEA
WITH BECCY'S FAVOURITE RECIPES

A step-by-step guide on how to host your own afternoon tea featuring Beccy's favourite recipes.

BECCY HUNT

www.chezbeccy.com

A Guide to Hosting Afternoon Tea
with Beccy's Favourite Recipes

First Edition

© 2024 Beccy Hunt

Beccy Hunt asserts the moral right to be identified as the author of this work

Photograph page 2 & 12 Emma Harrel
Photograph page 7 & 10 Stephanie Jansen
Illustrations by Beccy Hunt

All rights reserved. No parts of the publication may be reproduced, distributed, or transmitted in any form or by any means including photocopying, recording, or other electronic or mechanical methods without prior written permission from the publishers.

For any queries please email beccy@chezbeccy.com

Scan the Qr code for free recipes on the Chez Beccy Life You Tube channel.

(To scan the Qr code hold the camera on your smart phone over the Qr code and click then click the link that appears on your camera)

www.chezbeccy.com

CONTENTS

ABOUT BECCY 8

HISTORY OF AFTERNOON TEA 16

PLANNING YOUR AFTERNOON TEA 22

CREATING THE MENU 30

ALL ABOUT TEA 38

COLD DRINKS 45

SANDWICHES 48

SCONES 54

SWEET TREATS 58

MY NOTES 78

www.chezbeccy.com

www.chezbeccy.com

ABOUT BECCY

Welcome to Chez Beccy, where my passion for cooking and sharing delicious food with loved ones is at the heart of everything I do.

Food has always played a significant role in my life. My Mum is an exceptional cook. Her food philosophy is about using the best possible seasonal ingredients available, preferably homegrown from her impressive vegetable patch. If not homegrown, then organic and free-range options with minimal preservatives and additives are preferred.

www.chezbeccy.com

However, Mum wasn't much of a baker, and didn't particularly enjoy desserts and cakes, making them a rare and cherished treat.

Like many children growing up in the 1970s, I developed a love for cake and chocolate. Yet, the cakes available in England at the time were often overly sweet and filled with synthetic cream and covered in bright pink icing.

A pivotal moment occurred during a childhood family holiday when I discovered the delights of Cornish clotted cream. This experience opened my eyes to the joys of afternoon tea, and I've been hooked ever since.

My love of cream teas grew during surfing trips. Whilst I wasn't a great surfer, I loved the outdoors and would often be found in the local tea room sampling scones while my friends were catching a wave.

My culinary horizons expanded significantly when I left home at 18 and went to work in a Swiss ski resort. It was there that I experienced the most amazing cakes and desserts. On my days off I would visit the local bakery, sitting on the balcony overlooking the ice rink, indulging in heavenly hot chocolate and decadently creamy gateaux. It was also where I first tasted Bircher muesli—a truly incredible experience. To this day, I've yet to find a Tiramisu as exquisite as the one served at the Schweizerhof Hotel in Lenzerheide.

My time in Switzerland marked the beginning of almost a decade of travelling across the globe, filled with fascinating food experiences. Some were delightful and others not so much. During inter-railing trips around Europe, I had the pleasure of sampling incredible cakes and pastries in countries like France, Germany, and Austria. They were unlike anything available in English bakeries at that time. On one trip I stumbled upon an amazing baking cookbook in a German bookshop, which I still treasure and use today.

Chocolate, raspberries, and cream quickly became staple ingredients in my baking repertoire, inspired by the delicious treats I encountered during my travels. One of my favourites is the 'Vertical Layered Chocolate Cake,' which I am delighted to share the recipe with you here.

After many adventures I decided to settle down and pursue a more conventional life as a travel agent - it seemed like the logical career choice.

During this period, I realised I wanted to follow a creative path. Growing up I was always making things, whether it was building camps in the fields, making jewellery from pumpkin seeds to sell in my pretend shop, or completing the latest Blue Peter craft project. I decided to follow my passion further. I enrolled in college and completed an art foundation course followed by a degree in graphic design at Nottingham Trent University. Landing my first design job as a greeting card designer was a proud moment for me. I vividly recall the sense of accomplishment when I filled out a form for a Sainsbury's loyalty card, proudly listing my occupation as a designer. It was an exhilarating feeling!

Chez Beccy was born out of defiance. After a year of attempting

www.chezbeccy.com

to transition from greeting cards to homeware design, I decided to take matters into my own hands. I thought, 'Right, I'll just do it myself. How hard can it be?' It turns out, it was quite challenging! However, the journey has been incredibly rewarding, and I've grown to love all that comes with learning how to run a business.

I love being in my kitchen cooking and baking and my passion for homeware began when I bought my first home. I remember putting my collection of blue and white china on the dresser in

www.chezbeccy.com

the kitchen and realising that I wanted to create complementary blue and white kitchen textiles. It felt like the perfect finishing touch to complete the look.

I chose the name Chez Beccy because I envisioned it being more than just a kitchen textile brand. It's a lifestyle brand, inspiring everyone to find joy in their kitchen, enjoying good food, and connecting with friends, both old and new.

This year has seen the exciting addition of the **Scone Baking Demonstration with Afternoon Tea** events to the Chez Beccy calendar, where you can join me in my kitchen and I share the secret of how to bake the fluffiest scones and one other afternoon tea deligh, followed by a freshly baked traditional afternoon tea.

This book is all about embracing the joy of baking and hosting an afternoon tea. Delve into a brief history and the rise of its popularity in Britain. I will then guide you through the process of hosting your own spectacular afternoon tea party. From who to invite, downloadable templates for invitations and name place cards, to selecting a theme, considering table décor, every detail is covered. You will explore menu planning for mouth watering food and drink options, as well as my personal favourite recipes for the best sandwiches, scones and cakes.

To conclude, ample space is provided for you to map out your afternoon tea event and include your own delicious recipes.

www.chezbeccy.com

www.chezbeccy.com

Whether you're a seasoned chef or a novice in the kitchen, I hope to inspire you to embrace the spirit of afternoon tea and make it your own. Whilst there can be a lot of etiquette associated with afternoon tea, just have fun, make some delicious food, and enjoy it with your friends.

The art of creating a stunning afternoon tea lies in precision and attention to detail. Sandwiches are easy to make, and by getting the proportions right, you can create a taste sensation. A garnish will take your presentation to the next level! Scones are at their best when fresh, and cakes are cute as mini decorated cakes; a dusting of icing sugar always looks pretty.

Have fun creating joyful memories with friends and loved ones. And if, after reading this book, you decide this all sounds wonderful but *I'd much rather Beccy baked her delicious scones for me*, then I'd love to welcome you to Chez Beccy.

I am thrilled to share that there are more cookbooks in the pipeline. It's just a matter of deciding which one to tackle first!

Simply scan the Qr code below for more information.

Beccy x

www.chezbeccy.com

*"Life is like a cup of tea,
to be filled to the brim and
enjoyed with friends"*

CHEZ BECCY
HOMEWARE · ACCESSORIES

The History of AFTERNOON TEA

Afternoon tea is an essential and cherished part of English heritage, deeply ingrained in the cultural fabric of the nation. It is a tradition that transcends generations, bringing people together to indulge in a quintessentially British experience.

The ritual of afternoon tea embodies hospitality, reflecting the rich history and enduring charm of England.

It all began when tea was first introduced to England in the mid-17th century when Dutch and Portuguese traders, who had established trade routes with China, introduced this exotic beverage to the English elite. Initially, tea was a luxury reserved for the wealthy, admired for its rarity and novelty.

The Portuguese wife of King Charles II, Catherine of Braganza, was credited with popularising tea in England among the aristocracy. Its association with opulence quickly made it a sought-after symbol of status among the aristocracy and upper class.

Throughout the 18th century, tea became increasingly accessible as trade expanded, leading to the emergence of tea houses and coffee houses as popular social venues.

Despite its growing popularity, high taxes on tea prompted widespread smuggling and illegal trade during this period.

The 19th-century Industrial Revolution revolutionised tea production and distribution, making it more affordable and widely available to the general population.

Tea became deeply ingrained in English culture, evolving into a beloved national beverage associated with hospitality, socialising, and relaxation. Today, it remains an integral part of British identity and heritage, symbolising centuries of trade, social customs, and cultural evolution.

It is estimated approximately 100 million cups of tea are drunk daily in Britain!

www.chezbeccy.com

It was Anna, the 7th Duchess of Bedford, who is often credited with popularising the concept of afternoon tea among the aristocracy and upper-middle class in the early 19th century. Although the tradition of consuming tea and light refreshments in the afternoon pre-dates her.

As the story goes, Anna, feeling hungry in the late afternoon, began requesting a tray of tea, bread, butter, and cake to be brought to her room. She found this light meal refreshing and soon began inviting friends to join her, and so contributing to establishing the social ritual of afternoon tea.

Afternoon tea quickly became a fashionable social event among the aristocracy and upper-middle class. It was an opportunity for people to gather in the late afternoon to enjoy tea, delicate sandwiches, scones with clotted cream and jam, and a variety of

www.chezbeccy.com

pastries and cakes. However, over time, the tradition evolved to become more accessible, with people from all walks of life enjoying its delights.

As afternoon tea gained popularity, certain etiquette and traditions developed around it, including the proper way to brew and serve tea, the sequence of consuming food items, and the use of fine china and silverware.

These days, afternoon tea has continued to evolve to reflect changing tastes and lifestyles. Variations include themed afternoon teas such as champagne afternoon tea or afternoon tea with unique flavour combinations and contemporary presentation styles.

Overall, the history of afternoon tea is a fascinating journey that reflects the intersection of culinary tradition, social customs, and cultural evolution. It continues to be cherished and enjoyed as a beloved British institution, both at home and abroad.

*"Good luck is the result
of good planning!"*

-David Ignatius-

CHEZ BECCY
HOMEWARE · ACCESSORIES

PLANNING

Planning an afternoon tea party can be a delightful experience. This is a step-by-step guide to help you plan and host a memorable afternoon tea party. Follow these steps to make it fun and enjoyable for you as well as your guests!

The art of creating an amazing afternoon tea lies in precision, attention to detail and planning. Each element, on its own, is not complicated, but knowing exactly when to perform each task can help to alleviate any stress.

The most important thing is to remember to have a good time, and create beautiful memories with friends and loved ones.

PLANNING

SET THE DATE AND TIME
Choose a date and time for your afternoon tea party. Afternoon tea is typically served between 3:00 pm and 5:00 pm, but you can adjust the timing based on what suits you.

THE VENUE
Are you planning on hosting your afternoon tea party in your kitchen or dining room or outside? Think about how many people you can comfortably accommodate, how many people can you sit at the table, and how many place setting do you have?

CREATE THE GUEST LIST
Determine how many guests you'd like to invite and make a list of their names and consider the seating arrangements.

SEND INVITATIONS
Send out invitations to your guests well in advance, preferably 2-4 weeks before the party. Do you want to send traditional paper invitations, e-vites, or create a Face book event?

Scan the Qr code to download the afternoon tea invitation and the name place cards. Or copy the link below into your browser http://eepurl.com/hf-_h1

www.chezbeccy.com

Dear _____

YOU ARE INVITED TO

Afternoon Tea

Date _____

Place _____

_____

_____

R.S.V.P. by _____

www.chezbeccy.com

THE THEME

Make your event stand out by choosing a theme! Afternoon tea is the epitome of luxury, elegance, refinement so always bear this in mind when choosing a theme. It can be as straight forward as a *birthday party* theme, or you could have a seasonal theme such as *Easter* or *Spring* or just a *colour scheme*.

HOW TO CREATE YOUR THEME
There are three main categories you can think about here; colour, table decorations and the menu.

1-COLOUR
What colours sum up you theme? I would recommend using two or three main colours.

2-THE TABLE
What mini table decorations or table confetti can you use to enhance your theme. There are some fabulous options available, you can really go to town and have fun here!

3-THE MENU
Are there any particular sandwich fillings which will go well with your theme? Maybe there are some cakes or cake decorations that would be fun to have.

Don't forget to think about drinks. Hot drinks, cold drinks and what about a celebratory glass of bubbly?

www.chezbeccy.com

FOR EXAMPLE - AN EASTER THEME

The principle elements could be daffodils and tulips and chocolate eggs. Using bright spring colours such as yellow, orange and green.

Blue compliments the bright yellow really well, so consider how stunning a table laid with white china, blue & white cloth napkins and table runner, will look.

Simply scan the Qr code below to visit the ChezBeccy.com website and take a look at the beautiful table linen Collections.

A fabulous arrangement of spring flowers such as daffodils and tulips make a great centre piece for the table.

There is also an amazing selection of Easter table decorations available such as little yellow chicks, sheep and mini eggs, to delight your guests.

Consider continuing the Easter theme onto your invitations and name place cards to really wow your guests!

FOR EXAMPLE - A BRITISH THEME

An afternoon tea party is such a British occasion, and makes a really good theme, using red, white and blue.

An eclectic mix of blue and white china will look lovely on the table. In charity shops and antique shops you can find a great

www.chezbeccy.com

selection of vintage blue and white china. Mix the patterns and styles to create your unique look.

Red and white cloth napkins and a table runner can be used for the red element. (These are available from ChezBeccy.com)

A beautiful floral arrangement is a great way to enhance your colour scheme and bring everything together.

Red, white and blue bunting creates a celebratory atmosphere.

Paper table confetti of typically British icons such as Union Jacks and red London buses can be really pretty and is an easy way to elaborate on your chosen theme.

www.chezbeccy.com

Print place name cards for all your guests to they know where to sit. You can download and print these name place cards to use at your afternoon tea event.

Scan the Qr code to download the afternoon tea invitation and the name place cards. Or Copy the link below into your browser http://eepurl.com/hf-_h1

(To scan the Qr code hold the camera on your smart phone over the Qr code and click then click the link that appears on your camera)

www.chezbeccy.com

"I bake therefore I am"

CHEZ BECCY
HOMEWARE · ACCESSORIES

THE MENU

Decide on the menu for your afternoon tea party.
Keep it simple and luxurious at the same time.

Serving smoked trout and Champagne, Prosecco
or Cava is a great way to create an opulent
feel to the afternoon.

Seasonal touches add finesse, such as a bowl
of freshly picked summer berries.

Enquire whether your guests have any food allergies or
intolerances before they arrive so you are prepared.

THE DRINKS

TEA
It is traditional to serve loose leaf teas, English Breakfast and Earl Grey are good choices. English Breakfast Tea is a robust black tea that pairs well with milk or dairy-free substitutes. Earl Grey Tea is a fragrant black tea infused with bergamot oil, often served with a slice of lemon.

If you are hosting your afternoon tea in the summer, you might choose to offer something like Fresh Mint Tea as well.

COFFEE
Some of your guests may prefer coffee. A freshly made filter coffee in a cafetière will compliment the afternoon tea well.

BUBBLY
Serving a glass of bubbly will elevate the experience to a luxurious and celebratory occasion.

Prosecco is a sparkling wine from Italy known for its crisp and fruity flavour profile. Cava is a Spanish sparkling wine that offers excellent value and a range of flavour profiles from dry to slightly sweet. Champagne is the classic choice for celebrations, from the Champagne region of France known for its elegance and complexity. Whichever you choose, serve chilled in elegant flute glasses.

OTHER DRINKS
On a warm summer afternoon a Homemade Still Lemonade is a refreshing and nostalgic option, or you might opt for an Elderflower Cordial served with Sparkling Water, for a bit of fizz!

www.chezbeccy.com

THE FOOD

My favourite Afternoon Tea Menu Plan is on the page 34. Why not use this as a starting point to create your menu and amend to suit your tastes. When baking or cooking for other people I would always recommend you try out the recipe at least once before cooking/baking for guests.

There are three main elements to consider for the menu, the sandwiches, the scones and the cakes.

Always use the best quality ingredients that are available to you, it really can make a difference to the flavours. I prefer to use smoked trout rather than the more traditional smoked salmon as I believe it is farmed in a more sustainable way.

Afternoon tea is about attention to detail. As well as creating tasty treats, the food is best if kept small and delicate and the sandwiches cut into fingers or triangles with the crusts removed. The sweet treats work well as mini versions with beautiful little decorations. These small details will amaze your guests!

Cucumber and egg & cress sandwiches are both classic British options for an afternoon tea, so a must for me. And smoked trout elevates the occasion to something very special.

Scones can be plain or fruit and if you can serve these warm, straight from the oven for your guests, they will be a real show

www.chezbeccy.com

stopper! Make these just at the last minute so they are as fresh as possible. Cheese scones are also delicious but I wouldn't choose to serve them for afternoon tea. These are great for lunch, especially when served with homemade soup.

My three favourite cakes are on the sample menu. Delicious nutty almond financiers decorated with frosted fruits, meringue kisses with strawberry ripple cream and mini chocolate sponge cakes with a chocolate ganache icing.

The meringues can be made in advance as they keep really well, then they can be filled with the strawberry ripple cream on the day. Make the mini chocolate sponge cakes in the morning so they are lovely and fresh. Leave them to cool and then ice with the chocolate ganache so it has time to set before they are eaten.

SUPPLIES & EQUIPMENT

Make sure you have all the necessary supplies for baking everything you want to make, and ensure you use the right size cake tins as stated in the recipe.

Check the temperature of your oven is correct with an oven thermometer.

Ensure you have all the teapots, teacups, cutlery, crockery, glasses, cake stands, and serving trays, dishes, table cloth or table runner. Cloth napkins are always nice to use.

Simply scan the Qr code below to check out the beautiful selection of table linen at ChezBeccy.com.

www.chezbeccy.com

CHEZ BECCY

HOMEWARE · ACCESSORIES

MENU

DRINKS
Loose Leaf English Breakfast Tea
Loose Leaf Earl Grey Tea
A Bottle of Bubbly
Homemade Lemonade

SANDWICHES
Cucumber Sandwiches on White Bread
Egg and Cress Sandwiches on White Bread
Smoked Trout Canapé on Brown Bread

SCONES
Fruit Scones served with
Strawberry Jam and Clotted Cream

CAKES
Frosted Berry Financiers
Meringue Kisses with Strawberry Ripple Cream
Mini Chocolate Sponge Cakes with Chocolate Ganache
Bowl of Fresh Seasonal Berries

www.chezbeccy.com

PREPARATION

Plan your shopping. Make a list of ingredients you need to buy, equipment and decorations. Decide when you are going to do the baking. List all the other tasks that need to be done and make a note of when you will do them.

Prepare as much as you can ahead of time, to make it a stress free occasion. Is there anything you can make well before hand, such as make the Still Lemonade?

A FEW DAYS BEFORE
Do all shopping for the food and drinks. Prepare all the glasses, crockery, table linen, cake tins, utensils & serving dishes. Write a name place card for each guest.

THE DAY BEFORE
Bake the meringues and biscuits as these both keep really well in an airtight container. Make your frosted fruits as well. If you want to serve ice with your cold drinks fill up your ice cube trays and place in the freezer now. Put the cold drinks in the fridge to chill.

EARLY MORNING
Set the table with tea cups, saucers, teaspoons, plates, napkins, and any additional decorations you plan to use. Put a name place card on each place setting.

Arrange the tea selection, English Breakfast and Earl Grey along with the sugar. Put the milk into a jug and put in the fridge.

www.chezbeccy.com

Bake the cakes you have chosen to make so they have time to cool before icing and serving.

Prepare the cucumber, egg, and cress fillings for the sandwiches. Assemble the smoked trout canapés on brown bread. Keep these fresh in an air tight container in the fridge. If you butter the bread this will help stop the filling's moisture soaking into the bread and making it soggy.

LATE MORNING

Ensure you have strawberry jam and clotted cream ready for serving alongside the scones. Assemble sandwiches, cut the crusts off the bread and garnish with fresh herbs. Ice and decorate the mini chocolate sponge cakes.

MIDDAY

Bake the fruit or plain scones.

JUST BEFORE GUESTS ARRIVE

Arrange the cakes on serving platters or cake stands and decorate so they look irresistible.

Set out the scones with strawberry jam and clotted cream.

Prepare the Tea by boiling fresh water and put the loose leaf tea in teapots, ensuring you have enough hot water available for refills.

Welcome your guests and enjoy the party!

www.chezbeccy.com

"Tea is always a good idea"

CHEZ BECCY
HOMEWARE · ACCESSORIES

TEA

Traditionally afternoon tea is served with tea. Tea comes in many forms from green tea, black tea, white tea, oolong tea as well as herbal tea. It can be argued that there is nothing more refreshing in the afternoon than freshly brewed tea, whether you just make a cup of tea or go all out and brew a pot of tea.

Creating your perfect cup of tea is a very personal thing. We all have slightly different preferences. Whether you like a stronger brew, add the milk in first, have a slice of lemon, it's all about finding the perfect flavour for you! So when you are thinking about hosting an afternoon tea, you might want to consider catering for a few different tastes.

There is a fabulous variety of teas to choose from these days and most of them come from India, China or Sri Lanka.

Tea is made from the dried leaves of the plant, *Camellia sinensis*, an evergreen shrub and grown on plantations. The quality of the tea and the flavour is determined by many factors such as the time of year the tea is picked, the climate and altitude it grows at as well as the quality of the soil. Much like a grape will make a different wine every year, so will the leaves of the *Camellia sinensis* make a different tea every year.

In spring, the youngest two leaves and bud are hand-picked. These first picked tips are highly prized and known as the golden or silver tips. At peak harvest tea is picked up to two or three times a week!

Green Tea: Once picked, the leaves are *'fired'* straight away, which means the leaves are heated and gently rolled in a metal pan so they dry out. The heat stops the oxidation which inhibits the development of caffeine and preserves the antioxidants as well as the green colour.

www.chezbeccy.com

Black Tea: The most popular tea here in the U.K. First the leaves are *'withered'* which is a gentle drying process, then they are cut and torn by machine to open up the cells for fermentation. These blackened pieces of leaves are then dried again and finally graded by size. This results in the tea being fully oxidised, creating a higher caffeine content and the familiar golden brown colour.

Oolong Tea: Is half way between green tea and black tea. The leaves are partially fermented, resulting in more complex flavours than green tea and a beautiful fragrance. It is often referred to as a blue-green tea because of the colour of the leaves.

Tea Blends: These are produced by blending two or more varieties together. The most popular in the U.K. is English Breakfast Tea. This can be made from black teas from anywhere, of a reasonably high quality and has rather a strong flavour. This is most often drunk with milk.

Earl Grey Blend is a milder blend than English Breakfast Tea, flavoured with bergamont oil, making it more fragrant with a note of citrus. This is often drunk with a slice of lemon.

Lapsang Souchong is another of the more well known blends. Its distinctive smoky flavour is created by drying the leaves over pine-wood fires.

Chai tea is a spiced tea blend that typically consists of black tea brewed with a mixture of aromatic Indian spices and herbs. The exact blend of spices can vary, but common ingredients include cinnamon, cardamom, ginger, cloves, and black peppercorns. This creates a rich and fragrant beverage.

Infusions: Rooibos or Red Bush tea made from the leaves of *Aspalathus linearis* from South Africa, has become popular now, here in the U.K. The leaves and stems are picked and chopped to initiate oxidation and left to undergo natural fermentation which allows the leaves to develop the characteristic red/brown colour and distinctive flavour. It is high in antioxidants and caffeine free.

Herbal Teas: There are many herbal and fruit teas, often caffeine free as they are not made from the leaves of the *Camellia sinensis* plant and have medicinal properties. These are best made from the fresh plants, such as Fresh Mint Tea and Ginger which are both good for the digestion. Camomile tea is thought to be calming and aid sleep. There are many of these blends which are enjoyed mainly for the flavour.

Fruit Teas: Generally, they do not claim to have any of the medicinal properties of herbal teas. These are drunk purely for the flavour. It is useful to know that some fruit teas use black teas a base, therefore do contain caffeine.

www.chezbeccy.com

www.chezbeccy.com

THE ART OF BREWING TEA

Tea making is a key part of British culture. And like all the elements that go into creating a beautiful afternoon tea experience, it's the attention to detail that can make all the difference. Whilst there is an element of personal preference, there are some important details to note.

The favoured blend of black tea for a traditional afternoon tea is English Breakfast Tea and it has been made the same way since the mid nineteenth century.

Choose Quality Tea: Start with high-quality loose leaf tea. The type of tea you choose (black, green, white, etc.) will depend on your taste preferences. Also note, different leaves have different qualities. Green leaves may need a longer brewing time, you may prefer Earl Grey with no milk or a slice of lemon instead.

Use Fresh Water: Fill the kettle with fresh, cold water to boil for your tea. Avoid reusing water that has been previously boiled as it may affect the taste.

Warm the Teapot: If using a teapot or cup, warm it by rinsing it with hot water. This helps maintain the temperature of the tea for longer.

www.chezbeccy.com

Measure Tea: Measure out the appropriate amount of tea leaves or tea bags based on your preference and the strength of tea desired. Typically, one teaspoon of loose tea leaves or one tea bag per cup is a good starting point.

Infuse the Tea: Pour the hot water over the tea leaves and let it steep for the about 2-5 minutes depending on the type of tea and your taste preferences. Be mindful not to over-steep, as this can lead to bitterness.

Remove Tea Leaves: Once the tea has steeped for the desired time, remove the tea leaves from the teapot or cup to prevent over-brewing.

Add Milk and Sugar (Optional): If desired, add milk, sugar, honey, or other sweeteners to taste. Different teas may pair better with certain additions, so experiment to find your perfect combination.

Enjoy: Pour your freshly brewed tea into a cup and enjoy it while it's hot. Savour the aroma and flavour of your perfect cup of tea.

Remember, the perfect cup of tea is ultimately a matter of personal preference, so feel free to adjust the brewing time, tea-to-water ratio, and additional ingredients to suit your taste.

www.chezbeccy.com

COLD DRINKS

ELDERFLOWER CORDIAL

A quintessentially English summer drink, wonderfully refreshing and a perfect accompaniment to afternoon tea. Find out more about foraging on my Chez Beccy Life Blog

INGREDIENTS

15 Elderflower Heads
1 Litre of Water
500g Caster Sugar
4 tbsp of Runny Honey
2 Lemons

METHOD

Wash the elderflower, and take off any bugs.

In a large saucepan, put in the water, sugar and honey. Slowly bring to the boil and simmer until all the sugar has dissolved.

Remove from the heat and add the zest of 2 lemons and the elderflower. Make sure the flowers are completely covered in liquid.

Add the juice of 1 lemon and slice the other lemon and add as well.

Put the lid on and leave for 24 hours.

Strain the cordial by placing a muslin cloth over a sieve. If you don't have a muslin, use good quality kitchen towel.

Store in sterilised bottles. Drink diluted with water, sparkling water or Prosecco.

www.chezbeccy.com

STILL LEMONADE

Wow your guest with this wonderfully old fashioned drink that is making a come back now in contemporary tea shops and it's so easy to make!

Makes 4-6 glasses

INGREDIENTS
3 Unwaxed Lemons
125g Caster Sugar
900ml Boiling Water

METHOD

Peel the skin from the lemons with a vegetable peeler, in the same way you would peel and apple.

Put the lemon peel into a large jug.

Add the boiling water and stir until all the sugar has dissolved.

Cover and leave to cool.

Squeeze the juice from the peeled lemons and add the juice to the jug. Mix well.

Strain into a large glass jug and garnish with mint leaves and a few thin slices of lemon.

Serve cold, over ice.

www.chezbeccy.com

*"Happiness is amazing food
and great company"*

CHEZ BECCY
HOMEWARE · ACCESSORIES

SANDWICHES

Delicate sandwiches are the first essential component of any afternoon tea, providing a savoury balance to the sweet treats typically served alongside them.

These sandwiches offer a delightful burst of flavour in every bite. From classic cucumber and cream cheese to indulgent smoked trout and dill.

Additionally, the artful presentation of these sandwiches adds a decorative element to the tea table, enhancing the overall aesthetic appeal of a wonderful afternoon tea experience.

In essence, delicate sandwiches embody the essence of sophistication and refinement, making them an indispensable part of the cherished tradition of afternoon tea.

You might rightly think that you don't need a recipe to make a great sandwich! And to get that taste sensation, it's all about attention to details and the ratio of the filling and bread to wow your guests!

CUCUMBER & CREAM CHEESE

Makes 8 triangular sandwiches

INGREDIENTS

1/2 Cucumber, peeled
4 Slices of White Bread
100g Cream Cheese
2 tsp of White Wine Vinegar
2 tbsp Chives, finely chopped
Salt and Pepper
Unsalted Butter, room temperature

METHOD

Cut off the domed top part of the slice to make a square.

Trim the peeled cucumber so it's the same length as a slice of the bread. Thinly and evenly slice your cucumber length ways.

Mix the cream cheese, vinegar, chopped chives salt and pepper in a small bowl.

Lightly butter each slice of bread and spread on the cream cheese mixture.

Pat the cucumber dry with a paper towel and then arrange on top of the cream cheese mixture.

Sandwich together with another slice of lightly buttered bread.

Remove the crusts of the 3 sides and cut into triangles.

TIP

Use a mandolin to achieve beautifully even slices of cucumber, but do be careful of your fingers and use the guard!

www.chezbeccy.com

SMOKED TROUT

Makes 12 triangular sandwiches

INGREDIENTS

6 Slices of Wholemeal Bread, medium
Unsalted Butter, room temperature
100g Smoked Trout
3 dsp of Crème Fraîche (half fat or full fat)
1 Heaped tsp Horseradish Sauce
A Squeeze of Lemon Juice
1 tsp Finely Chopped Fresh Dill (if you have it)
Freshly Ground Black Pepper

METHOD

Butter the bread, and cut off the domed top part of the slice to make a square.

Mix the crème fraîche, horseradish sauce, finely chopped dill, freshly ground black pepper and a squeeze of lemon juice together.

Place a layer of smoked trout on 3 of the square slices of bread.

Then spread the crème fraîche & horseradish mixture generously all over.

Sandwich together with the another slices of square bread.

Remove the crusts from the remaining 3 sides and cut into triangles.

TIP

Smoked trout is available from all good supermarkets and fishmongers. I use medium sliced Hovis wholemeal bread.
Place the butter in the warming draw of the oven to soften so it is really easy to spread and doesn't break up the bread.

www.chezbeccy.com

EGG & CRESS

A wonderful old fashioned English sandwich filling. My granny would makes these. She buttered the loaf of bread before she cut the slice so she could cut really thin slices!

Makes 8 triangular sandwiches

INGREDIENTS

2 Eggs, the best quality available to you
4 Slices of White Bread
2 dsp of Mayonnaise
A Bunch of Cress, finely chopped
Salt and Pepper
Unsalted Butter, room temperature

METHOD

Boil the eggs for about 9 minutes until hard boiled. Allow the eggs to cool and then peel.

Cut off the domed top part of the slice to make a square and butter the bread slices.

Place the eggs in a bowl and chop roughly. Stir in the mayonnaise, the cress, salt and pepper. Mix together and spread onto 2 of the slices of bread.

Sandwich together with another slice of bread.

Remove the crusts and cut into triangles.

TIP

Place the butter in the warming draw of the oven to soften so it is really easy to spread and doesn't break up the bread.

www.chezbeccy.com

HAM & MUSTARD

Makes 8 triangular sandwiches

INGREDIENTS

Unsalted Butter, room temperature
4 Slices of Wholemeal Bread
4 Fine Slices of Roast Ham
English Mustard, to taste
Salt and Pepper

METHOD

Cut off the domed top part of the slice to make a square and butter the bread slices.

Place a layer of finely sliced ham on top of 2 the slices of bread.

Spread over the English mustard, to taste and seasons with salt and pepper.

Place another slice of ham on top and other slice of buttered bread.

Remove the crusts from the 3 remaining sides and cut into triangles.

TIP

Place the butter in the warming draw of the oven to soften so it is really easy to spread and doesn't break up the bread.

www.chezbeccy.com

*"A scone with jam and cream
is heaven on a plate!"*

CHEZ BECCY
HOMEWARE · ACCESSORIES

SCONES

Scones are best served freshly baked and still warm from the oven with strawberry jam and clotted cream.

Whether you prefer fruit or plain scones they are an essential component of an afternoon tea menu and offer a delightful contrast to the delicate savoury sandwiches of the first course typically served during afternoon tea.

However you choose to serve the scones, they are a comforting indulgence that perfectly complements the ritual of tea-drinking.

With their timeless appeal, scones embody the essence of refined elegance in the afternoon tea experience.

SCONES

Delicious plain, with fruit or cheese!

Makes 14-16
Use a 5½ cm round cutter.

INGREDIENTS

500g Plain Flour
A Pinch Salt
2 tsp Bicarbonate of Soda
4½ tsp Cream of Tartar
75g Cold Unsalted Butter, diced
300 ml Milk
1 Large Egg, beaten

OPTIONAL

75g Raisins or Sultanas for Fruit Scones
65g Mature Cheddar and 65g Parmesan for Cheese Scones

METHOD

Preheat the oven to 210°C/190°C Fan.

Sift the flour, salt, bicarbonate of soda and cream of tartar into a bowl. Rub in the cold diced unsalted butter.

If you want to add cheese or dried fruit, now is the time to do that. Then add the milk all at once and mix lightly with a spatula.

Then knead the dough with your hands in the bowl until it all comes together as a soft dough.

Turn out onto a floured surface and knead lightly again. Roll out to about 3 cm thick.

Cut out the scones and place on a baking tray lined with baking

www.chezbeccy.com

parchment. Brush with the beaten egg. If you're making cheese scones, sprinkle with grated cheese. Cook for 15-20 minutes or until risen and golden.

Best eaten straight away!

TIPS

When rubbing the butter into the flour, shake the bowl and the larger pieces of butter will come to the top of the bowl. Also make sure you incorporate all the flour at the bottom of the bowl.

Try not to work the dough too much as this is the key to light and fluffy scones.

Dip the cutter into the bag of flour before cutting out each scone so they don't stick to the cutter.

Be very precise when measuring out the milk. If you use too much milk the dough will be very sticky and the scones will be flat.

You might want to check your oven is the correct temperature with an oven thermometer

www.chezbeccy.com

*"Good things come
to those who bake"*

CHEZ BECCY
HOMEWARE · ACCESSORIES

SWEET TREATS

Cake, pastries and biscuits are an indispensable element of any afternoon tea, adding a touch of sweetness and indulgence to the tea table.

These decadent treats, often in miniature form, adorned with icing and beautiful decorations, serve as the perfect finale to the elegant afternoon tea.

The variety of cakes and pastries offered during afternoon tea allows guests to indulge in a symphony of flavours and textures, from rich chocolate ganache to light and airy sponge cake.

Indulging in these sweet delights creates a sense of celebration and adds an element of joy and festivity to the timeless tradition of afternoon tea.

FINANCIERS WITH FROSTED BERRY

Makes 12

INGREDIENTS
150g Unsalted Butter, plus extra for the tin
175g Icing Sugar, plus extra to serve
150g Ground Almonds
50g Plain Flour
4 Egg Whites (freeze the yolks for another recipe)
2 tbsp Flaked Almonds

FROSTED FRUIT
Seasonal Soft Fruits such as Raspberries, Red Currants, Blueberries (a few leaves, like mint if possible)
1 Egg White, Beaten
Caster Sugar
Icing Sugar for Dusting

METHOD
Preheat the oven to 200°C/180°C Fan/Gas mark 6.

www.chezbeccy.com

Melt the butter in a saucepan over a medium heat until it starts to foam. Continue to cook for 4-5 minutes until small bubbles start to appear – the butter should be golden brown and smell nutty. Remove from the heat and set aside to cool slightly.

Mix the icing sugar, almonds and plain flour in a large bowl.

Whisk your egg whites for a few minutes until a light foam appears on top. Then gently stir into the dry ingredients.

Gradually mix in the butter (making sure to include all the little brown specks that are packed with flavours!) until smooth.

Cover and leave to rest (for 20 minutes).

Carefully spoon the batter into the moulds as evenly as possible. Sprinkle the flaked almonds over the top. Then bake for 15-20 minutes until firm to the touch and golden.

Leave to cool for 10 minutes before carefully turning out onto a wire rack to cool completely.

FROSTED BERRIES

Rinse the berries and any leaves in cold water. Then pat dry with kitchen paper towel.

Place the caster sugar in a shallow bowl. Brush each fruit, stem and leaf with a light coating of beaten egg white and place into the bowl of sugar. Roll in the sugar, completely coating each piece and place on a wire rack to air dry until the sugar has set. You might want to place some baking paper underneath to catch any drips.

To serve arrange the frosted berries on top of each financier and dust with a little icing sugar.

www.chezbeccy.com

TIP

Make the frosted fruit the day before so it has plenty of time to air dry.

It's worth investing in a Silicone 12 Cup Mini Loaf Cake Tin for this recipes.

Beat the egg white well as this will make your financiers really light.

Turn the tray around in the oven, half way through cooking for even baking.

NOTES

www.chezbeccy.com

MERINGUES KISSES
WITH A
STRAWBERRY RIPPLE CREAM

Serve these with an extra bowl of strawberries and raspberries along with plenty of whipped cream!

Makes 24

INGREDIENTS - MERINGUES
2 Egg Whites
100g Caster Sugar

RIPPLED CREAM
250g Strawberries, hulled
25g Caster Sugar
2 tsp Cornflour
175ml Double Cream

DECORATION
Fresh Mint Leaves
Icing Sugar for dusting
Mini Berries

www.chezbeccy.com

METHOD

Preheat the oven to 100°C/80°C Fan/Gas mark ¼

Crack each egg and separate the egg whites into a mixing bowl.

Whisk until the eggs white double in volume and form a peak when the whisk is run through them.

You can do this with an electric whisk or a food mixer.

Then start to add the sugar a spoonful at a time, making sure each spoonful is fully incorporated before adding the next.

Whisk until all the sugar has been added and the whites are glossy.

Take a sheet of baking parchment and draw 3½ cm (ish) circles using an edible pen. (An up turned icing nozzle is about the right size). Draw 48 circles on 2 sheets of baking paper each on it's own baking tray.

Place a dot of meringue mixture in each corner of the baking tray so your baking parchment will stick to the baking tray and not move around.

Spoon the meringue into a large piping bag with a plain nozzle and pipe 48 mini meringues. Start in the centre of each circle and squeeze the piping bag until you reach the edge of the circle, then stop and pull the piping bag up and you will have a lovely round meringue with a little peak.

Do this 47 more times until there is no more meringue mixture left.

Bake for 3 hours, turning the baking tray around half way through the cooking time, until they are crisp and easily lift off the paper. Leave to cool.

www.chezbeccy.com

THE STRAWBERRY RIPPLE CREAM

Chop the strawberries quite small and place in a saucepan with the sugar and cornflour. Cook over a low heat, stirring all the time, for about 10 minutes until you have a thick strawberry sauce. Leave to cool.

Whip the double cream until it forms stiff peaks and then fold in to strawberry sauce. It looks nice if the mixture isn't completely mixed together so you get a rippled effect.

Place a spoonful of the rippled cream onto 24 of the meringues and then sandwich together with the remaining meringues to create your delicious meringue kisses. Add little fresh mint leaves to decorate and dust with icing sugar.

Arrange on a plate with more mint leaves and a selection of mini berries.

TIP

Meringues keep really well for a few days in an air tight tin, so can be made in advance, then fill with the rippled cream and add the decorations just before serving.

To get beautifully white meringues you need to cook them in a cool oven for a long period of time.

You could also substitute the strawberries with raspberries.

NOTES

www.chezbeccy.com

MINI CHOCOLATE SPONGE CAKES

Makes 10

INGREDIENTS- CHOCOLATE SPONGE

3 tbsp of Boiling Water
25g Cocoa Powder
2 Large Eggs
115g Unsalted Butter, softened
105g Golden Caster Sugar
75g Self Raising Flour
1 tsp Baking Powder
A Pinch of Salt

CHOCOLATE GANACHE

50g Dark Chocolate
50g Milk Chocolate
100ml Double Cream

DECORATION

Fresh Raspberries
Small Fresh Mint Leaves
Icing Sugar for dusting

www.chezbeccy.com

METHOD

Preheat the oven to 200°C/180°C Fan/Gas mark 6.

Grease a loose bottom 12 cup mini sandwich tin. Cut the butter into cubes and place somewhere warm to soften.

Sift the cocoa powder into large mixing bowl, then measure in the boiling water and mix together.

Add the eggs, soften butter and sugar to the bowl. Then sift in the self raising flour, baking powder and salt.

Beat together scraping down the sides of the bowl as you go, incorporating all the ingredients fully.

Divide the cake mixture evenly between 10 cups. It's about 3 teaspoons of mixture per cup. Leave a gap of about 1 cm at the top of each cup and smooth the tops off with a teaspoon.

Bake on the middle shelf in the oven for about 13 minutes. When cooked, a skewer inserted into the middle of one of the little cakes will come out clean and the top of the cake will be springy to touch.

Leave for a couple of minutes to cool down in the tin, then place each cake onto a wire rack to cool completely.

THE CHOCOLATE GANACHE

While the cakes are cooling make the chocolate ganache.

Break the chocolate into small pieces, put in a saucepan, then add the cream. Bring to the boil, take off the heat and whisk until you have a smooth icing.

Cut the cooled mini chocolate sponge cakes in half horizontally.

Take a heaped teaspoon of the ganache and place in the middle of the cake in the centre. Smooth off with the back of a spoon.

Then place heaped teaspoon of the ganache on the top of each little cake in the centre and smooth over. Decorate the top of each mini cake with a fresh raspberry and a small mint leaf. Dust with icing sugar just before serving.

TIP

Be careful not to over bake these cakes, it's worth investing in an oven thermometer to check your oven is the correct temperature.

NOTES

MINI CINNAMON BISCUITS

Makes approx 32 mini biscuits
Use a 4½ cm round cutter for mini biscuits, which are just right for afternoon tea.

INGREDIENTS
200g Plain Flour
¼ tsp Salt
½ tsp Cinnamon
½ tsp Mixed Spice
100g Unsalted Butter, cut into cubes
100g Golden Caster Sugar
50g Currants or Sultanas
1 Egg, beaten
Caster Sugar for sprinkling

METHOD
Preheat the oven to 180°C/160°C Fan/Gas mark 4.

Place reusable non-stick baking tray liners on 2 baking trays.

Measure the flour into the bowl. Add the salt and spices. Then rub in the butter.

Stir in sugar and currants.

Beat the egg and pour into the bowl with the dry ingredients.

Start to bring together using a spatula and then your hands. Knead lightly in the bowl until it all comes together as a soft dough.

Chill the dough if it's a bit sticky. If it's too dry and crumbly add

www.chezbeccy.com

a little cold milk to bring it all together into a smooth dough.

Sprinkle a little flour on your work surface, and knead the dough lightly.

Roll out to about 5 mm in thickness. Cut out biscuits and place on a baking tray. Sprinkle with caster sugar.

Bake on the middle shelf in a preheated oven for 15-17 minutes or until pale golden-brown.

Place on wire rack to cool.

NOTES

www.chezbeccy.com

PEANUT BUTTER COOKIES

Makes approx 28

INGREDIENTS

285g Plain Flour
½ tsp Baking Powder
½ tsp Bicarbonate of Soda
A Pinch of Salt
115g Unsalted Butter, room temperature
230g Crunchy Peanut Butter
175g Golden Caster Sugar
115g Light Soft Brown Sugar
1 Large Egg
1 tbsp Milk
1 tsp Vanilla Extract
150g Unsalted Peanuts, in halves
Golden caster sugar for sprinkling

METHOD

Preheat the oven to 180°C/160°C Fan/Gas mark 4.

Place a reusable non-stick baking tray liner on a baking tray.

You will need a large and a medium sized mixing bowl.

Sift the flour, baking powder, bicarbonate of soda and salt into the medium sized mixing bowl.

Put the butter and peanut butter into the large mixing bowl and beat together until fully incorporated. Now beat in the golden caster sugar and the light soft brown sugar.

www.chezbeccy.com

Now beat in the eggs, vanilla extract and milk. An electric whisk works well here. Don't forget to scrape down the sides of the bowl to fully incorporate all the ingredients.

Then add all the dry ingredients and the unsalted peanuts.

Mix together with a spatula to start with, then use your hands to form a dough.

Take a spoonful of dough, approx 40g if you want all your cookies to be the same size, and roll into a ball with your hands.

Place each ball into the baking tray, leaving plenty of space for each one to expand into as it cooks. Press down lightly on each ball of dough with a fork to flatten them, they will be approx 5 cm across now.

Bake on the middle shelf of the oven for about 15 minutes, until they begin to firm up and are slightly golden in colour.

Leave to cool on the tray for a few minutes to harden and sprinkle with golden caster sugar. Then transfer to a wire rack to finish cooling.

NOTES

www.chezbeccy.com

VERTICAL LAYERED CHOCOLATE CAKE

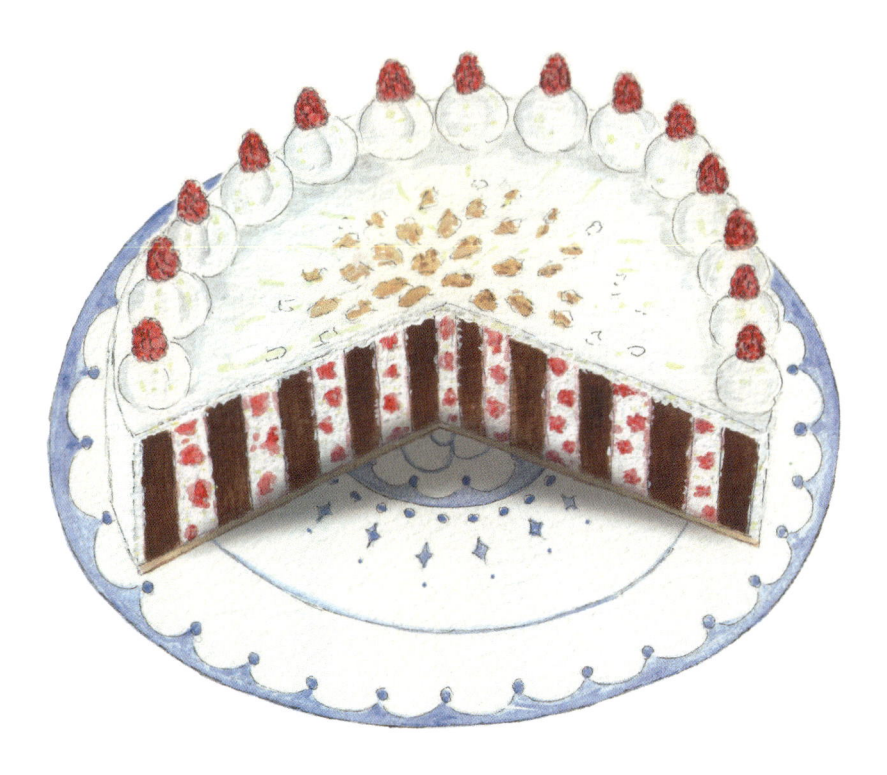

This is a real show stopper! It might seem complicated but it's just 3 parts put together to make a statement piece. You can make the shortbread base the day before and once the chocolate Swiss roll is made, it's just a matter of assembling it!

www.chezbeccy.com

INGREDIENTS- SHORTBREAD BASE

100g Unsalted Butter, room temperature
50g Caster Sugar
150g Plain Flour

CHOCOLATE SPONGE

4 Eggs Separated, plus 2 Egg Yolks
100g Caster Sugar
80g Plain Flour
25g Cornflour
35g Cocoa Powder

RASPBERRY CREAM FILLING

450g of Fresh Raspberries
15g Powdered Gelatine
450ml Double Cream
70g Icing Sugar

DECORATION

250ml Double Cream
1 tbsp Icing Sugar
25g Flaked Almonds

METHOD

Make the shortbread base first. Cut the butter into cubes and beat together with the sugar until light and fluffy. Sift the flour and stir into the butter and sugar, then work into a round ball of dough. Wrap in tin foil and leave in the fridge for 2 hours.

Preheat the oven to 220°C/200°C Fan/Gas mark 7.

Grease 23 x 33 cm Swiss roll tin and line with greaseproof paper. In your largest mixing bowl whisk all the egg yolks together with half the sugar until thick and creamy.

In a medium sized mixing bowl whisk the egg whites until stiff,

www.chezbeccy.com

then whisk in the rest of the sugar. Now fold the egg whites into the egg yolk mixture.

Sift the flour, cornflour and cocoa powder onto the egg mixture and fold in using a metal spoon. Make sure all the ingredients are fully combined.

Pour the mixture into the Swiss roll tin and spread out evenly to the corners.

Bake for 10-12 minutes. Sprinkle sugar onto a piece of baking parchment. Turn the sponge out on top of the sugary paper. Remove the lining paper from the base of the cake, cover with a damp tea towel and leave to cool.

Turn the oven down to 190°C/170°C Fan/gas mark 5.
Grease a 20 cm round loose bottom cake tin. Roll out the ball of shortbread into a circle to line the tin. Bake for 15-20 minutes and leave to cool in the tin.

Keep a handful of raspberries aside for decorating the top of the cake. Lightly crush the rest of the raspberries.

Dissolve the gelatine into 3 tablespoons of cold water over a gentle heat.

Pour the cream into a bowl and sift in the icing sugar, then whip until stiff. Fold in the cooled gelatine and the crushed raspberries.

Spread the fruit and cream mixture evenly over the sponge and cut lengthways into strips about 5.5 cm wide.

Place the shortbread base onto the cake plate. Now roll up the first strip of chocolate sponge with the fruit and cream filling and stand upright on the centre of the shortbread base.

Take the next strip and continue to fold around the central roll forming a spiral until you reach the edge of the shortbread base.

Place the cake in the fridge to set for about an hour.

www.chezbeccy.com

Whip the cream and the icing sugar together to decorate the outside of the cake.

Cover the top and the sides of the cake in the whipped cream, smoothing with a palette knife. Pipe rosettes of cream on the top of the cake to decorate along with the raspberries. Finish with a sprinkling of flaked almonds.

NOTES

www.chezbeccy.com

NOTES

www.chezbeccy.com

"There is always time
for tea and cake!"

CHEZ **BECCY**

HOMEWARE · ACCESSORIES

MY NOTES

Now it's your turn!

Make this your own afternoon tea bible, where you can create your perfect afternoon tea experience. Have fun with the planning and be creative with your theme.

Jot down new recipes here and note down those top tips that will make your tea party unforgettable.

Let your creativity flow, and let's make some delightful memories. Bon appetit!

www.chezbeccy.com

AFTERNOON TEA

DATE

TIME

GUESTS

INVITATIONS

Scan the QR code to download the afternoon tea invitation name place cards and blank menu. Or Copy the link into your browser
http://eepurl.com/hf-_h1

THEME NOTES

___

___

___

___

___

___

___

___

___

___

___

___

___

www.chezbeccy.com

SHOPPING LIST

www.chezbeccy.com

MENU PLAN

DRINKS _____

_____

_____

_____

FOOD _____

_____

_____

_____

_____

_____

_____

_____

_____

_____

_____

_____

_____

www.chezbeccy.com

CHEZ BECCY
HOMEWARE · ACCESSORIES

MENU

DRINKS

SANDWICHES

SCONES

CAKES

www.chezbeccy.com

TO DO LIST

THE DAY BEFORE

ON THE DAY

WHAT WENT WELL?

WHAT WOULD YOU DO DIFFERENTLY NEXT TIME?

www.chezbeccy.com

NOTES

www.chezbeccy.com

AFTERNOON TEA

DATE

TIME

GUESTS

INVITATIONS

Scan the QR code to download the afternoon tea invitation name place cards and blank menu. Or Copy the link into your browser http://eepurl.com/hf-_h1

THEME NOTES

_____
_____
_____
_____
_____
_____
_____
_____
_____
_____
_____
_____
_____

www.chezbeccy.com

SHOPPING LIST

MENU PLAN

DRINKS _____

_____

_____

_____

FOOD _____

_____

_____

_____

_____

_____

_____

_____

_____

_____

_____

_____

_____

_____

www.chezbeccy.com

CHEZ BECCY
HOMEWARE · ACCESSORIES

MENU

DRINKS

SANDWICHES

SCONES

CAKES

www.chezbeccy.com

TO DO LIST

_____

_____

_____

_____

_____

_____

_____

_____

THE DAY BEFORE

_____

_____

_____

_____

_____

_____

_____

_____

www.chezbeccy.com

ON THE DAY

WHAT WENT WELL?

WHAT WOULD YOU DO DIFFERENTLY NEXT TIME?

www.chezbeccy.com

RECIPE

INGREDIENTS

DIRECTIONS

www.chezbeccy.com

RECIPE

INGREDIENTS

DIRECTIONS

www.chezbeccy.com

RECIPE

INGREDIENTS

DIRECTIONS

www.chezbeccy.com

RECIPE

INGREDIENTS

DIRECTIONS

www.chezbeccy.com

RECIPE

INGREDIENTS

DIRECTIONS

www.chezbeccy.com

RECIPE

INGREDIENTS

DIRECTIONS

www.chezbeccy.com

www.chezbeccy.com

RECIPE

INGREDIENTS

DIRECTIONS

www.chezbeccy.com

www.chezbeccy.com

NOTES

www.chezbeccy.com

NOTES

www.chezbeccy.com

NOTES

www.chezbeccy.com

ACKNOWLEDGEMENTS

I would just like to give a huge thank you to all my wonderful friends and family who support me in all that I do. Especially Jim, who is my rock and grounding force. Mum and Dad, whose culinary expertise has been a boundless source of inspiration. My sister, Anne-Marie, for her unwavering support as well as Gillian, my lovely Mother-in-Law, for her encouragement.

To my dear friend, Laura, who inspires me to keep going and whose editorial insights have greatly enhanced this book. A special thanks to her daughter, Katie, for her invaluable input. My wonderful friends Heidi, Polly and Wendy for their enduring support. Marea, whose encouragement was instrumental as I embarked on the journey of entrepreneurship. As well as Amanda, Ieva and Saj for their encouragement and inspiration along the way.

To Elif Köse, my business mentor, whose guidance and inspiration have propelled me forward, enabling me to achieve so much including the completion of this book.

Your support, encouragement, and belief in me have been the driving force behind my accomplishments. Thank you from the bottom of my heart.

www.chezbeccy.com

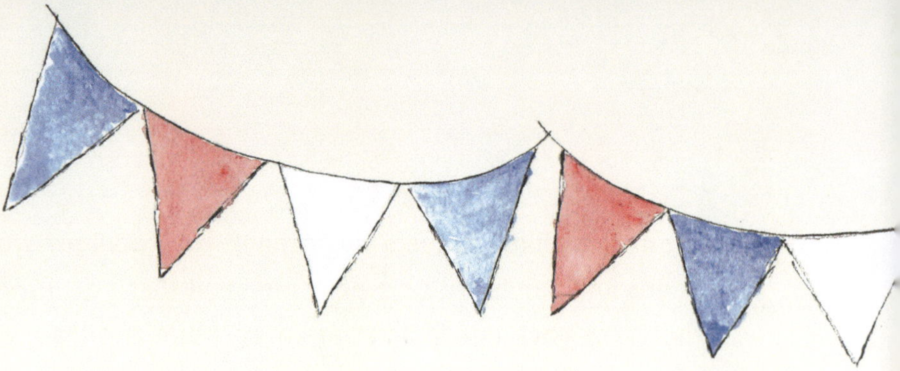

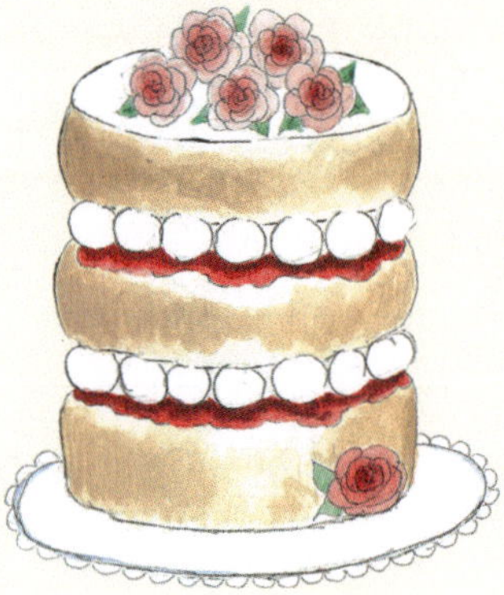